LOTUS GATHERERS

Amali Rodrigo was born and grew up in Sri Lanka. She has lived in Mozambique, Kenya and India, and is now based in London, researching a PhD while working as an associate lecturer at Lancaster University. She won the *Magma* judge's prize and second prize in the *Poetry London* poetry competition, both in 2012, and has been highly commended in numerous others including the Bridport, Ballymalore International, Montreal International and *Wasafiri* poetry prizes. Her first collection, *Lotus Gatherers*, was published by Bloodaxe in 2016.

AMALI RODRIGO

Lotus Gatherers

BLOODAXE BOOKS

ISBN: 978 1 78037 287 7

First published 2016 by
Bloodaxe Books Ltd
Eastburn
South Park
Hexham
Northumberland NE46 1BS

www.bloodaxebooks.com
For further information about Bloodaxe titles
please visit our website or write to
the above address for a catalogue.

Supported using public funding by
ARTS COUNCIL
ENGLAND

Printed in Great Britain by Bell & Bain Limited, Glasgow, Scotland, on
acid-free paper sourced from mills with FSC chain of custody certification.

For Sanya

ACKNOWLEDGEMENTS

Acknowledgements are due to the editors of the following publications in which many of these poems and translations first appeared: *The Poetry Review*, *PN Review*, *Magma*, *Moth*, *Poetry London*, *Wasafiri*, *Modern Poetry in Translation*, Café Writers Poetry Competition website and *Bridport, Montreal International Poetry Prize* and *Paeleton* anthologies.

My debts are many in completing this book, but I owe special thanks to Roddy Lumsden, Bill Greenwell, Graham Mort, John Glenday and Conor O'Callaghan. For *Aftersongs*, warm thanks to Ian Duhig, for his generosity and incisive reading of the complete manuscript of translations, and Neranjana Gunetilleke for sourcing reference material. My warm appreciation to Heike Benz and Jon Sayers, for their friendship and cheerful support over the years. I am grateful to my family always, for their love. This book is for Sanya.

CONTENTS

The lotus-eaters did not enchant you with the honey taste of forgetfulness. They safely slipped from their myth while you and your kin entered the labyrinth unprepared... You know exactly what you left behind.

MAHMOOD DARWISH, *The Presence of Absence*

Kāma Sūtra

Think of the weaver bent over the loom
in a posture of appeasement, though it is not.
He hears the beyond in him, an older voice.

Without pause or trembling, his winged
hands thread the shorter weft of cerise,
silver, through warp taut on its frame.

Though he does not pause, think of the rain
he doesn't miss, pounding on the roof,
branches of the jacaranda scratching

the windowpane like a cat impatient
to be let in. Think how they learn
to wait, as all things must,

while the foliage thickens, until a hare
finds itself startled by a star or the deer
occasionally leaping. In a quiet opening

a hunt is taking shape. Though he doesn't
know where each turning may lead,
he adds lilies, a monkey like a go-between

among the banyan's sky-roots, a peacock
unhooking its nerve. Think how he breathes
into them, into each knot reworked,

each new loop that shows a little more
of itself, and this archer, he sends
into the world to become an arrow.

When all the birds fly up at once
in the tapestry's very centre,
think of the barely disturbed tree.

Lotus Gatherers

As if a glasshouse god made:
in its centre

small miracles
men moon-walk towards

at dawn, chest deep
in broken open

water and a wake
of slurred silt.

As they near, the thousand
watching eyes

are a clatter of stones
on glass

that find no saviour
within earshot.

This is the clear water
where lotuses have always lived

in benediction
and safekeeping. If they heard

rumours of a far shore,
they thought nothing of it.

So they wait, faces clear,
not knowing how

to forfeit roots,
gill buds, or turn away

from their own harvesting's
delicate work,

this terrible
tenderness of platonic

hands, that they absent
themselves

from themselves like glass
eating glass.

Meditation on Cherry Blossoms

When the first buds open in Okinawa
it is not a joy exactly.
The snow has not stopped for days.

Even when it does, I listen
each night to the blossom forecast
and think only of snow falling.

        *

On the day they told us of a change in Kumamoto,
I saw how I had changed between the beginning
and the end of the sentence.

        *

How earnest the wind is, through cracks
in floorboards, roof tiles. Then it is tongue-tied for so long
I think the world has died.

        *

There are days you want to know the truth so badly
you'll trade anything for it.

When they announce the blossoming in Kyoto
I want to take it all back.

        *

A bridge between one shore and the other –
the river forever trying to escape it.

This is how longings arrive: with tiny buds
of resolutions that will not survive.

        *

Down by the river the trees are raucous
in bloom, the wet road beneath marching
steadily towards the house.

        *

The dog's tail thumps and thumps
on the floor. He watches a door
that never opens.

*

Blossoms always return to the same tree.
In my dream I return to the same house,
yet that road is unrecognisable.

*

I wake night after night
to unspooling distance,
and the blossom's steady earthshine.

*

Knowing true North, how lightly they travel
right through us to Nagoya.

Blindly we offer ourselves
to the spaces we are made of.

*

When they began to bud in Aomori, at the ocean's brink
I understood how desire has enormous scales –
is like fish leaping in our bodies.

When they began to bud in Aomori
they were also waiting to ignite in Hokkaido,
Okinawa, Aomori and for a second

I believed I was here, I was real.

*

When they began to bud in Aomori, I understood
what I am to you is a mirror
that says you are beautiful.

*

When the first blossoms appear in Hokkaido
it is like something breaking far away.

Good Luck Goldfish

To generate the most luck, use nine fish:
eight red or golden and one black.

FENG SHUI

Where there is water there is a memory
of a river, of a chalice, of a thirst
unslaked. Here, among amulets
and totems, inside a display case, the Koi
run frantic in their small silver cell
as if the force of desire could recover
the river, red flecking water, water turning
to wine. How shall I drink such blunt ardour,

such clockwork blessing. A vagrant gene
turned gold. Yet the source is here
too, a barely visible gravity we keep
arriving at, wanting happiness, exacting
its due. Finding how every paradise is walled,
we make our own way home, hearing the river near.

Something Borrowed Something Blue

A vow: the cosmos
            of a dandelion

delirious
            beneath a breath

on the brink of

The Bell Is Always Ringing

If, to hear is a long
gathering's interruption
of *this this this* –
not *tongling* bronze,
not the iron cast heft
of a house, not a *zhong* bell's two
exact tones, but perhaps like
someone caught
in a small act of love,
or the trace of a day he held
a hint of her at the far end
of a hallway, she, panicking
out of sight in a blur
of bridal white,
and how smug
they were of reflex
superstitions:
the anecdote pealing
through the intermittent
years – a coup,
until they find
themselves again
in an identical corridor,
like small clappers trapped
inside a clay *ling*, diasporic
chime of an elevator
born again and again
in the muffled interior
of the hotel, rising high
or falling to the earth –
pint bell, quart bell, a hundred
weight bell, the crystal one
with a river in it,
sundering.
How deep then the grain
in walls, anonymous doors
branded by numbers,

the affluence of light
that cannot mark a time of day –
night-watch, harvest, or wedding feast.
And spangles in lush pile,
as if only just risen
into being around the bare
toes puckering
into it.

Kintsugi

There comes a time when a lingering
brightwork is the only *tell* of love
beyond platitudes of *the radiance*

of fractures, that *brokenness*
is a blessing etc.
Imagine a monk's devotion

on pilgrimage, divested of all
but his robe and bowl, thinking only
of kneeling at an invoked chapel.

A heartland, he finally enters
to find old consolations no more
or nourishing. But the chapel stands

for eternity, is a round world
that can be cupped in a palm
and filled with meat.

For now, he'll walk ley lines like cracks
on clay, the touching points
that make each fragment among another

relevant, a necessary extension.
He'll even pause at a crosswind
on a high curve and find no battle site,

no cairn where a want was set straight
on its path; but tributaries, flowing secret
and bright, that have no ocean to give

out at and no birthing spring.
I had not known how I believed
in a durable self until I saw, in mending,

a void amassing in the bowl.
What a vessel may hold, be the measure
of. How it sings.

How like a body, it sits apart
among kindred, and is safe to use.
How my arms went dead

holding it to your mouth
for your lips to open
and eat.

Bamboo Flower

I've listened so long in terrible thirst
to the suck of my sap, rising and rising
in culms scaling towards the sun.

Words well and set in pale
nuggets, heavier each passing year.
Which is worse: to be unheard

or live unable to speak?
What came to me daily was wind
whickering about hollow

chambers, the tap-tap
of a bamboo-cutter's knife.
The instant I abandon prayer

it is answered. In a voice hoarse
with disuse I try to muster
a flower's grace –

bold, fluent, our cries race
across the land. Yet bees flee
from us, there is no delicacy

in our monologue, no nectar,
or perfume. It embarrasses
me to bud. But the world listens

as our single offering of seed
is homing in on vagrant winds.
Are we the lucky ones when

it's the dread of a ruined world
that opens hearing
to our first words, first light?

Satī

All things are far

RILKE

Who are these women like birds of paradise,
dancing with smoke from a nuptial hearth,
a love-match of feet against earth and rushing spirit –

Yet a *truth*, a *goddess* and a *fine-woman* are far
from each other, as a word chafed down
to gist, is as indifferent as fire

to what it consumes. A *truth* drawn glowing
can be cast into anything. At the crematorium
when grandma passed, sister whispered *potatoes* –

when she burns, we'll smell them boiling.
As a child I believed goddesses were signal
fires at our furthest hinterlands and wind,

the faithful runner keeping our histories
safe. But often it is just a woman you see
like a lantern moving through the night

of her given name, in delicate negotiation
to slip past its bars into a world without
end. *Satimata*, so nearly a goddess

if she lies down without weakening
while fire unbolts what life shut out.
Does faith come then on quiet feet?

Is there no place she can remain?
From a distance, the white of her stole
flowers into mirror-work, and the air is dancing.

This dawn, a pyre that starts from an unseen
corner. This ash, flaccid and spent.
This smell, no one wants to navigate.

Durian

I offer you my love like durian fruit,
thorn covered husk split with the knife

gripped in both hands, my full weight
into it, which gives, after its first resistance.

I do this outside, a good way from the house.
Two pale moons like *yes* and *no*

I sink my hands into, wrist deep,
snug fit of flesh, still hard and full with seed.

I ease out each stone, large as three knuckles,
gather white flesh untouched by green sap

and bury the husk to leave no trace of it,
wash myself twice at the well and carry it in,

drizzle cream, sugar crystals. The even scattering
of small pink bruises the thorns left on my palm

has almost faded when I offer you this
and you look as though I'd brought ambrosia.

Alms to Crows

Some things become such a part of us that we forget them

ANTONIO PORCHIA

They arrive all day in obsidian cloaks and slicked-back hair,
and wait with the eyes of misers, impatience of sages,
their cross-talk like sitars with broken strings.

Inside, mother and I boil rice in coconut milk.
We pat warm palmfuls into spheres, set them orbiting
on a platter, light a clay lamp in its centre. She tells me

crows are celestial messengers made of dark matter
shaped only by their containing vessels of air
and light, that crows are inside us all like blind spots

or retinal scars, behind our seemingly clear sight.
She's handing me a lexicon of the old ways we make
a game of – a madrigal feast for crows, their annihilation

of pearly planets of ill-fortune. Beneath the dark
gyres of their exodus, in deep quiet, we are
augurs reading claw-script on the ground.

The Fish

Community Panchayal directs rape accused to marry victim
Press Trust of India, November 2004

She can remove her bra and panties
beneath the tent of a *salwar kameez*, without
an inch of skin made visible.

She lowers her gaze in the presence of strangers
reads their feet like palms; cracked, pampered,
shod or barefoot.

She wants a husband whose feet
are not split at the heel like her father's
or caked in mud like her brother's.

1 Month Later:

Her husband-to-be has feet smooth
as de-scaled fish. The astrologer says
her firstborn will be 'famous'
I think they mishear 'miracle'.

Her family hears of a girl
who hanged herself by a *dupatta*; they hide
all of hers. She drinks gallons of milk,
the way the *Shiva Lingum* is cleansed
at temples. Her bridal sari is red.

The priest blesses them with a coconut, scatters
rice for fertility – he wasn't to know I am hiding
in the darkness inside her. She thinks his feet
are like newspaper parcels of fish,
faces sticking out, nails like flat fish eyes.

He takes her home with him that night.
His fish-feet mount hers.

I'm only a few cells along, but I know
something isn't right

from the way she stares at his feet.

3 Months:

She leaves all his shoes in the sun
to rid them of their fish and cabbage smell.
She eats a bag of figs, then pistachios,
then walnuts and retches with such force

that I'm afraid
of being wrenched free of her.

Her mother comes to take her back home.
It doesn't last long because all day her father
mutters like a prayer –
what will the neighbours think.

Before she leaves, she sneaks her old *dupattas*
from the linen cupboard in with her clothes.
No one sees what she takes away with her.

I swim in pumice when she scrubs her feet.
In this house, the smell of fish doesn't go away.

Big Fish Little Fish she murmurs to herself as she scrubs.

5 Months:

She turns sixteen today.
I don't hear voices. Maybe he is mute.
I have not seen his face, but I would

know his feet anywhere.

7 Months:

I give myself vertigo looking at feet
upside down. I sleep curled
the way she does. We are like seahorses.

I give myself vertigo again, doing hand-stands
to see the sky

when she cries outside on mangosteen-coloured nights,
we hang like bats from the sky.

His little toes are always turned sideways
for the weight of him.
The big toe has wiry whiskers on the knuckle,
like cat-fish.

The sound of fish breathing. Wet sound of fish kissing.

3 Days Before My Birth:

My mother can't sleep because I space-walk
inside her. She says:
The stench is unbearable and gets out of bed
(he is asleep).

She returns with the axe set apart
for cracking coconuts.

I must bury the dead fish she says,
looking at his feet.
I must bury the dead fish.

I am almost a miracle.

I Think of a Very Large Mechanical Mouth

when I discover Mother hunched
over the machine, face shell-pale,
making my ghost   so nearly
the sum of my parts.

She's feeding it yards and yards.
What passes for wings become arms,
from bare plains, a trunk. A hatch
for a neck, pipe for a leg.
She says all she has to, in sequins

and button holes. Sometimes she calls
me over. I thread the needle.
If I dared, I'd speak in silver bells,
the ones she tucks in rows on wrists.
Instead, I give myself over –

the deep inlet of armpits,
the narrow ladder of spine, dragon
work of bone and for years I wait
for stitches to spring, to touch my
nakedness, to find little medals of teeth

marks on skin, the machine's hum at the back
of everything, as if it was trying to tell
me something even as I was hoisted
by the heels and slapped
for a breath.

Wood-drift

There's wish to offer shelter
made good in great woods,
in the unshakeable church,
mast of an unsinkable
ship or wood gazing
into calm rooms
from rafters for years
and years – then
take to wandering
when houses fall
or bridges are replaced –
roving canals, streams
with the dumb rub
of cigarette butts,
rusted nails
milk teeth, a barge
for seed pods
river rats, molluscs –
longing to be
done with
yet finding no close
coast, stripped
and stripped,
taking the small role
the sea offers
to be left alone, go
only with a memory
root-deep, be wave
spun, be tally sticks,
squall formed
and once
or twice harbour
beside a boat,
wood to wood
looking up
at a parabola
of sky opening,

closing,
when one ebb
tide arriving
ashore bewildered
supplicants
less broken
than holding firm
tinder's thirst
for flame.

Ossuary

All calque, seething babble,
gnarly grey, ballack and gaw.
One bone fell upon another
as a loved body deranged,
femur to humerus, mandible
to radius, to lie apart from faint
quakes of loincloth spill, tinsel
voices gone inside out, as if
small hands of ash dropped
through skin into salt longings.
Tears, blood, deep stoppered
gush come to rest – us all
in some other tongue
heart calmed stallions
hush hush.

from **AFTERSONGS**

AFTERSONGS are based on the medieval graffiti 'song-poems' inscribed at Sigiriya, Sri Lanka. Sigiriya is a royal pleasure palace and fortress built by the patricidal King Kashyapa, in 5th century CE. The palace stood on the summit of a sheer 200 metre rock. One flank of the rock is believed to have been decorated with approximately five hundred frescoes of 'cloud maidens', 20 of which still survive. After the king's death in battle, Sigiriya was converted to a Buddhist monastery and later abandoned. The identity of the women has been fiercely debated ever since Sigiriya was rediscovered in the 19th century.

Placed below the frescoes is the highly polished 'mirror wall' where visitors to the abandoned palace inscribed ekphrastic song-poems. The majority of inscriptions date from between the 8th and 12th centuries. So this dialogue spans more than four centuries.

Nearly 1500 complete poems or poetic fragments have been deciphered to date. The language is medieval Sinhalese, or *Eḷu*, a more erudite register that does not admit Sanskrit *tatsamas*, or loan-words. It is an unstressed language. Although ten syllabic metrical systems have been identified, *Yāgi* is by far the most common. It is a metre that falls easily into the speech rhythms of the language, much like iambics in English.

It is remarkable that many of the writers seem to have conformed to the contemporary aesthetic standards for verse, although only two have explicitly identified themselves as poets. Others are from diverse backgrounds and occupations such as a bookkeeper, a drummer, an ironworker, a physician, a superintendent of the slaves, Buddhist clergy, members of royal households etc. Only a handful of verses are by women. Many song-poems contain a didactic, Buddhist, metaphysical subtext that contrasts strongly with an open sensuality in others.

Another significance of the graffiti song-poems is the device of dialogue or *uba-bas-lakara*. This is not recognised in classical Sanskrit poetics and is believed to be an indigenous development. *Ubabas* in relation to *ekphrasis* – giving voice to silent works of art as a poetic device – wasn't to develop in other world literatures for many centuries.

34

On this desolate mountain,
young and doe-eyed, she lifts
a string of pearls and stares
as if she's better than I.
O the fury in me

– A woman

My friend has worn his blue robe
with an embroidered trim of scarlet
hibiscus to climb the mountain –

O the enchantment of breasts
like swans, tipsy
on the nectar of lotuses

Girl, isn't it enough that you quarry
our secrets, must you stiffen
us too with longing?

How glorious, this heaven's
nymphs lazing on a knoll –

can a man be blamed for the hand
that leapt to unhook a girdle?

How long she stares, tear-glazed,
down this rough road
fucked again and again in men's minds –
this is all she'll ever know of love

As a fleeing deer may pause
to turn towards its fear –
in the vast thicket of her grief
she smiles

This lovely woman unsnarling
her long black hair
went to her moonstone mirror,
and became the listless shadow
within, unable to break past
this world's membrane

Midway through the climb, fulfilment looming, I was blind
to the great suffering
that stood beside my desire

    Dawn breeze
    the scent
    of lotuses

    In the mansion of an awakened mind
    hearing is a door. Guard it with diligence!

    O how my whole being quakes
    at the deluge of a woman's smile
                           – *Novice monk*

The man whose lust is rewarded
by this gold-skinned girl – isn't he as one
who, having warmed himself by the fire,
lays down his head in it?

    Cast among glowing coals,
    gold too shall melt

    As an areca tree flourishing near water
    may yet set roots further afield,
    O faithless ones, you'd live in a ruin
    though a mansion's near
                – *Buddhist friar*

How clearly the way here revealed itself –
yet to leave – where is that path?

To have your soul lanced
by their loveliness
is like offering your own head
to a mahout's jewelled hook

        I rescued a single flower
        from my wife's robe and dropped it
        beside the gold-skinned woman
        and went swiftly away

As a lamp's wick formed of lightning,
desire splits the grief-stricken mind.

O friend, your wife dead,
know they are spectres
not women who hold their tongues

        You are as dew
        on a lotus petal.
        Knowing this men are drawn
        and bewildered
        at its loss
                 – Buddhist friar

        Art lays bare the nature
            of consciousness –
      a strand of curling hair – and the infinite
            stirs the mind
                 – Buddhist friar

The figure of the woman is excellently sketched –
this hand, this eye so alive. Yet no one
can give them utterance

The women on the massif
pour lightning's brilliance –

how does the painter endure
his great affliction?

He unpeels our minds
layer upon layer like a banana tree
seeding each find in his art.

Yet woman, your mind
is the single failure to find heartwood
in that tree

Pome of glamour
and a pit for a heart –

your radiance is
even a woman's muse
                    – *A woman*

You brag about your stylish verses
pilfered from another's musings –

when the golden peacock steps out to dance
the black sparrow too shall reel on the grass!

I groped, found only the rough
wall beneath my palm –

how could I have won a heart
from such a violation?

Eons on this rock
knowing a desirable man
shall never come

(A cloud maiden)

Taking a sapu bud in her hand
she bent my mind like a stalk

I am Sela Boyi, I wrote these two verses:

A flower revealed a woman's mind,
and a god-king's trodden by a mere man.
Such loveliness is now all mine to reign!

Ah you think much of yourself my man
as a bull shoots loose when the harness slips
supposing he too can clap and dance!
                                    – Wife of Sela Boyi

Wife, ever present, ever virtuous
how unlike this wild gust
of gold and grace
that uproars the mind

Husband! Have you been spurned?

It's a fine thing indeed to say
we can be happy again!
                                    – A woman

Behind the sweep of yak-tail fans
a jewel-flicker of eyes –

yet I too am a woman prettified
by gold necklaces
                – A woman

O long eyed one, I am the breeze
trembling your moonlight

Have you seen the woman in a silk sari?
Dropping a blue jewel into her bosom
she said, *whoever speaks belongs to me!*

As a lotus appears fuller
beneath an autumn moon,
she grows more distant
in our awe.

We turn away like the gluttonous bee
who traps himself in a tuber
and stings the indifferent
filament to spite its own fate

We head back in deepening
silence; theirs, ours, reconciling
                              – Prince Apa

When evening falls and I'm far from here
gold-skinned girls and the lily coloured one
shall be luffa buds tangling in butterfly pea

O you halfwits! The toil of four men
to compose a single verse and none
among you thought to woo a girl
the simpler way, with warm
rum or molasses!

– A woman

Monkey Trap

Because hunters know there's no rough handling
a monkey from its high perch, because they
know that to devise the best spell, they must
use mischief in themselves, they gouge a gap
in coconuts, just large enough for a hand
to slip through, but not for a sweet flesh-filled
fist to be withdrawn. But who can blame
these jealous gods of upper air? We, being
earthbound, have long prepared for the ripe gold
clusters suspended above us, have imagined
their sweetness spill and gather. *How close*
you say, you, who hear me deeply. I am
the void your hand passes into. I feel
every finger like five kinds of hunger
you are trying to hold or master again
and again. I let you, and I am fed.

Eagle Eating a Flamingo

Sweetheart, stop

    this patient picking
        through knick-knacks.

The flamingo is pink
    inside and out.

        You will love again.

Waiting for the Axe to Fall

Wind and rain like axes honing selves
on whetstone, and a vigil through chinks
in drawn blinds. At night, I console

my mind like a mad aunt in the attic
with a tray of quinces and small
knives. She turns her back on me again,

does not stop lancing ants on toothpicks. I leave
and go to bed. When an axe falls thousands
of miles away, I am deep in REM but something's

there all day, a misdirection like a hare's
dash and me staring at the spot it broke
through, convinced that one lost axe bred another.

I change the locks, wait out days, a cocked
gun. The pond freezes, unfreezes, nothing ever falls.
I take to near-forgotten childhood games:

If a rook sits on the oak, the axe will fall today
or I play dead, a kind of truce, a kind of feint.
I do this for years before I remember the shed

where one was certain to be hung, and stalk through
bramble's raised stakes, past the stump with a zodiac
of nicks. Inside, something flew, something fled.

All I found was a naked nail, spiders retooling
fly traps and a slaking outline of rust – a face
pressed against glass for a minute – undone mote

by mote by ants like God's understudies and me
still standing there, a thin wire of blood from testing
a blade, begging them to stop, begging for another.

Bom Bom Bom Bom
Bombay Meri Hai

I look up from rubble and ruin and find a giant
Jenga tower as if the Djinns were at it again,
playing a drunken game by the swimming pool.
The pool is a spill of Blue Curaçao. The moon is
a raised tequila shot and white loungers, heaped,
is salt   on a mount-of-Venus ready for a lick.
Hookah puffs of cloud drift serenely by.

Party Hard drivers pace and bicker like house
sparrows by the gate. Rum-sloshed air makes
everything sticky, the night is amber-pretty.
High up, a midnight blue Djinn finger tap-taps
a window, carefully dislodges the brick. It is an
apartment complete with miniature couples,
children safe in match-box beds, ageing parents,
Ganesh statuettes, dream-twitching golden
retrievers on Kashmir carpets, camphor scented
Benares silks, moth-eaten mementos, and Louis
Vuittons still nested in tissue.

Everyone's tiny desires and fears bob free for a
moment like speech balloons as each brick is
safely misplaced. The tower grows taller, honey-
combs, but does not yet fall in a heap on the
marble forecourt. From inside some bricks, a
babble on astrology, eschatology, particle physics.
From others, stock market ticker-talk, CAPEX,
futures and cashflows, or a bass throb and the
ditzy stars of a mirror ball. The tower brims,
sharply focused as a Djinn's *Manhattan* tipping
into the invisible mouth, a fat maraschino cherry
somehow, somehow staying afloat.

Okapi

They said we'll never find them,
capricious as hearsay

or dream creatures, moving through
the forest like faint recollections,

a puzzle of pelt and form as if a child's
hand had a part in it, the myth

more perfect than a long low note
of an oboe or the russet of marrow

caved in bone, makes it necessary
to strike out on narrow trails

perpetually circling back or leading
to cliffs, where tracks fade

on the brink of space. The Okapi
disappears the way wind moves,

leaving no vacancy, the stilling leaves,
the coffers of light we can do nothing

with, that we grow into the listening
stance of a tree, and it finds us out

shoring up against a loss
that isn't there.

Happy Valley

(Kenya)

O Ra Ra Ra of days   hurrah the *mandjet*   stalled in our heavens.   Suckling
on bling   of salt on lips   on margarita flutes   kingfisher flash of air   around
the pool   we lie   ships run aground   resting where we lodge   skewed with
sun and slumber   slow-grilling   to the blush   of langoustine   glowing
of butter-melt   rocked by small quakes   of Pekinese Poodle and Pug   ecstatic
at slack leashes   getting it on   on lounger legs   while the Chihuahua   sails
downwind   maydaying   into a pyramid of shade   lets out a gurgled bark
a turd of gold   at finding instead   a looming dorsal.   All afternoon   flowers
say to the bees   ravish us for our sins   and the sun turns jade   with kingfishers.

Making Candles

Before the war years, as if I'd sensed
something at my back

aged seven, alchemist, seeker of light
I cracked the morning eggs myself

easing off their crowns, sabre-toothed
mistakes filled with delicate focus, insides

coaxed out through narrow gaps,
washed clean, here was my cask of light

when beginning of all things were candle stubs
and crayons boiled in discarded tins,

tiny explosions unleashing flecks of reds
and greens, I'd pour this hot tallow

to bury the wick; its genome twist
of twine tied to a matchstick balanced

on the lip of each egg-well, then the wait
for candles to harden in their moulds.

They say a candle flame makes a million
diamonds every second yet

no none knows what a flame
is really made of. This was when I found

that the wild gambit of dark
on the wall was only my body against

a stutter of old light and diamond
dust, monstrous, undefined

and the candle's shadow draped at its own
feet seemed most like betrayal.

Kolmanskop

(a ghost town)

I was sun-blind and listening to the sound of water
in wind, in desert sand, water in everything but

the river or the low trough where horses once drank
the sky. What survives is a tiny archipelago of wrecks,

the river an artery that bled out and out, became
an emboss of bone and I want to ask you if you truly

believe it is brave to enlist in war that is like the distant
sound of water with its cryptic messages of *a safer world*.

Thinking of you entering airspace, anonymous over sleep,
to leave trails of diamonds on the earth in one burst

of creation and your getaway mistaken for a star's blink,
can I forgive that you can't tell apart fleeing from stalking:

people beneath your bombs or prospectors straggling
across a desert to Kolmanskop driven by legends

of diamonds the size of men's hearts on riverbeds, as if
the milky way was laid down on earth for the picking?

From your great height you can't see how they lope alike,
mile by blistered mile, emptying of words, bearings –

some to find anyone who will save them, others not believing
they were only passing through, building houses, great halls

for opera now filling with wind's arias – men moving
too swiftly for the earth's slow kindling of diamonds.

All mined out, night in a ghost town is an armoured hood
with its shrapnel of stars. Soon you'll come, my wish,

my safe passage to a mythic lode, I too will say nothing,
taste the fine brine of your sweat, drink every cup of sand.

Glacier Lagoon

You were born in one country and will die in another
LI-YOUNG LEE

And here it is, the sound of things falling apart,
its ice-grind and rumble –

small clues passing unnoticed
or sifting into other sounds – snow geese

ticking overhead or a boat's distant grumble,
until continents give way in great heaves

and the earth trembles underfoot.
In the meltwater, cast-offs

half drowned and bare to the sun, open
sky-trapped blue hearts, everything they once

were, dripping away like refugees
learning a new language,

unable to shake off the foot-fall
of an old tongue. Floes drift, hang

back at the river-mouth, shape-shifting
hour by hour to the sea's low calls

beyond the parapet of sand, and resist
becoming one simple thing.

How to Watch a Solar Eclipse in a Bowl of Water

(Kandy, Sri Lanka, Insurgency 1987-1989)

> The unbearable lightness of being no one
> SLAVOJ ŽIŽEK

By day, stay close to home
    speak in modulated tones.
If the paper seller's son is gone
    don't ask after him.
Smile at the vegetable man's daughter
    even if you wonder – was it she
who slips *hartal* notices
    beneath coconuts, carrots?

Night after night
    let the house disappear,
the town
    with it the island.
Beyond the sea
    you may sense a lit planet
but know this darkness,
    how demarcations
are undecided.
    Lose your bodies
and live in voices.

Experiment with dumbness
    of hands, faces.
Scale dark hours with words
    learn the patois of silence,
its hesitations, swift leaps.
    Marvel
you are seventy per cent water, yet
    how easily you combust or float.

Like hunters beside night-fires,
    predators at bay
hush-hush
    tell tales, if only
of what you've heard –

how everyone stays away
    from the river,
after a raised arm
    in the murmur
drew eyes to those rocking
    downriver
like felled trees.

Outside, frangipani, verbena
    are at their most potent.
Breathe in these nights.
    Hope
to find no proof of anyone
    hula-hooped
in tyres and set alight.

It is your metronome of breath
    and winged gaze
like Minerva's owl
    that makes you real
without
    your animal body.

It is the world – trapped –
    that shatters again
and again
    in the skin of water.

The Eye

wants to be flung at everything, because it can
haul back or hoard, what's tugging to escape.

When its slow accretion like bric-à-brac
on a windowsill foreshadows the give

and take of a view, the Eye learns to high-step, turn
bird shaped. Sometimes it believes

in the eye of a Great Skua, who dives and dives
at intruders near nests, always missing the trick

of a raised hand; that the most visible part
of a thing, is not necessarily its weakest, nor all.

The Eye wants to hang back in a time
when bombs were new, pictures, uncensored

when a severed arm would not be replaced
by a bloodied shirt. Now, when smoke mushrooms

on skylines, Eyes fall to earth in great numbers, stagger
everywhere, half relieved they can't undo

what they don't have eyes to see. Sometimes
the Eye dreams of being a white elephant, rare

and auspicious, but is often fated to a vigil
on the sidewalk listening for a clink in the cup.

The Eye yokes itself to another to find depth
in the world, now and then, the calibration off-shot

as though through tears, it can't keep
from emptying all at once. The Eye is helpless

to stop the dilating iris from yielding
to remnants of light and sometimes, all it wants

is to be the gull that dips into the arched dark
beneath a bridge, and never comes out.

Peace

(Sri Lanka, 2011)

Within weeks of war's end, women everywhere began to find teeth marks on their breasts and bellies, often on the tenderest parts of their upper arms. Some woke to it after a restful sleep. Some were roused past midnight, finding no cause, turned over a new leaf of sleep. Days passed. Each found an echo of a narrative but no memory. Each found, how this confluence grew into a naked man, slathered in black grease, all of him faintly glistening as he moved like a night-river. They named it the *Grease Devil*.

In naming, this singular pain grew worse, so did the devil's ardour and night after night blood tie-died their sheets. Village men banded for vigilante night watch. Clutching at shadows, all they ever came away with were blackened, slick palms. Often there wasn't even that. If sometimes, a woman found flecks of skin beneath her own fingernails, she thought nothing of it.

One night, when they were all out to lasso this night-river, memories found them staring downstream with arms upraised as if in praise or supplication or surrender. When they came to, no one could tell which. But they sensed peace.

I could say peace was a river with time on its hands or a white elephant escaped from memory. I could say peace was stubborn as a water buffalo or shy as a sun-basking snake noosed in grass. But it wasn't like that. Peace waited all night to take in the faithless lover. Peace cursed like a fishwife brimful of toddy with her man so much at sea. Peace was less a woman with bitten breasts, though even now, some claim otherwise.

Origami

I stayed up all night folding the house,
the lotuses, the muntjac – edge to edge
the careful alignments, curves stripped

from form, a world of the straight
and narrow and oh so light. This page,
and all the rest I've given my best

to square up, unequal lengths cut away,
smoothing over old folds that marred
new sheets in my efforts

at difficult shapes – the identical
geometry in the face of the child
and the old man before details

are coloured in. I listened to diagonal
talk on discarded newspaper boats –
conversations that may never

happen elsewhere, the unsayable jutting
like wrecked masts and everything
unsaid inside the folds of a crane

or boat, and cranes do not lift off
into the calico sky, boats blunder,
papier-mâchés in an inch of rain,

the house still peels down
where it stands, inside me
entire cities are collapsing

without a sound, the world
weighed down by this
papery feeling.

Meditation on Cherry Blossoms

How simple the way sorrow
buds the body with air
and can't be exhaled enough.
How it overlooks
the old world – a temple's sky-bent
gables, every good luck
drum, prayer wheel – and horizon
to horizon a wild abandon
of permanent passing we come to
lie beneath again, full of days
when the universe seems a boastful child
with the new satchel and shiny pencil case,
when the days are prised open by *uguisu*,
mejiro, intent on one token half lost
in snow. Leave the world to birds.

We are long past ceding this want
of a bud to turn away from their preying,
the want to be held simply
on stem-warmed sap, making days
provisional. When centuries fret and fall
silent, there are earthbound shadows
to hunker in. And deep among the wilting
stars of the voice of a beloved
is a thing too softly uttered
but heard in the heart.

Ikebana

I must confess I doubted
the buds, these blade-edged
little bowls of vividness
prospecting gaze and heart.

So I took to the custom
that claims the way
of nature is three-pointed,
scalene – earth:human:heaven.

It teaches the grace
of a hard ground's yielding
to seedpods, flourish of leaf,
the meek grasses' impeccable

measuring of the world,
mosses that keep to themselves,
always looking inward
even as they increase,

and the naiveté of branches'
endless reaching out for firmament.
Much as I have loved
the commotion of blossoms,

poised here as a ladder
that knows its root and rest,
it is nothing compared to the star
that drops its late cargo

into a new night – it never demands
to be looked at. Think of it.
You have fed, walking alone
through deep blue on a strange lucidity

that only the absence of light
and sense of all the world dulled
by sleep, can illuminate. You have
felt the next closest thing

to your own attendance, not
human at all, but a vast gaze
that diminishes, not you,
but a quiet grief you've carried

since a child, and can't quite name,
and only recognise from its ebb.
Don't believe I am wooing you
if I give you a flower. It is merely

a token that darkness is truer
than light, it is a cue to a place buried
deep within us which refuses
to be harmed even by our passing.

Little Ghost

Every time we make love to a person, we create a little 'ghost',
an echo, a psychic imprint that will reverberate through time.

TANTRIC BUDDHIST BELIEF

What memory hungers
for is shelter, to inhabit
distances like swaddling

in a crèche of tallow light,
and a hope of some secret
fidelity, past long wandering,

to find the foundling
of our own bodies, both
sacrament and covenant.

Meteor Shower

And now in age I bud again
GEORGE HERBERT

The last fixed thing I saw, a fall of ash and moth-wing,
    not ready for old hungers and

your whisper in the pure dark: *like sperm racing*
    towards a cosmic egg.

Once we were plunderers, now lost, as if scratching runes
    on stone in this virtuosity of skin on skin,

all shapes burn and break – fingertips in tiny voids
    of dimples and folds, a palm over

the rib's insignia are the habit of knowing one thing
    through another, and a day long ago

when night rain barely hung on spruce boughs,
    their constellations marooned, trembling

like every tenderness in which a man can vanish,
    the body extinct, the who of it

as now, the body no longer a seed-silo, not yet an urn
    of ash but a pure toll of an ancient singing

bowl from us, padded hammer on lip, endless circum
    -navigation, a single note ransacking

the furthest reaches. This late in life we are
    younger than the river, older than the sky

Horology

For weeks, the on-off
thrum of migrating
geese overhead, then a hush.

All winter, children tick
inside houses,
sap draws trees to bone.

Elk, high-stepping
at the forest's edge,
are unaware

of becoming another's
illusion, conjured the instant
a deep run on snow

is found. Somewhere
someone is praying
in the shadows

while elsewhere another
is dancing: cog to groove,
like grief like joy,

the hour hitched to a wheel
turns and turns on itself,
as when we rested

this morning
breath to breath
and worlds apart.

It's the pivot points I'm after.
Some nights I dream
of entering the purled core

of a clock, side-stepping
seconds, the spring
of minutes,

as if there was a way
to master this art
of the diminutive –

then, it must be here, atomic
seconds, meeting points,
escape hatches, it must

be here, the pivot
of reasons,
of chance, of seasons,

or the grafted light
from a near forgotten touch.
This afternoon

a blood-call or some
absentmindedness
had a raven arrow low,

hurtle at the open door.
The eye of a dying bird
too is full of the world –

a miniature fixed on a grain
and perfectly portable.
Wherever it came from,

wherever it meant to go,
the day fills with a prolific
silence and a hunch

that it is always winter
somewhere, mirror after mirror
of opening.

Flying Over the North Pole

You think it'll soon be over, the cadmium
hinterland of ice beneath a domed sky, sea frozen
mid swell, everything in patterns of what was.

Here, the sun does not rise or fall but lists
on the horizon scattering pomegranate seed
and lemon peel on a white platter, and if being alive

is to be in motion, our great speed is imperceptible,
almost imaginary, with nothing but air and light
to measure our passing. A gaze can stutter

on such still life. It can fall back upon itself. To find
a slender china-crack of deep water is relief.
It's a navigable tract through a fixed hemisphere

and there far below, something else is alive, two
blue shadows in slow but clear progression
– perhaps whales sonar-navigating to warmer gyres.

Imagine how it is to breathe there, rising and rising
to crack a glassy crust, locked on the one route
through, the riddle of distances unravelling

like counting of each flake of snow as it falls.
Later you wake, having moved on, yearn to hold
on to what you can't make out or return to,

like the coriolis effect of seeing you again, perhaps
the whales were nothing but some inward call.
Now, our shadow is thrown back on to the ice

like a fly entering an old master's arrangement
of objects, tripping after the one constant thing –
when light was exact, its ceramic gleam unflawed.

Malum in se

Be mindful of the blade you have fashioned;
it is love and not a scourge.

ST UMILTÀ OF FAENZA

Between here and there
the fly is a knuckle rapping
and rapping   exiled
from the moist knife blade,
torn apples like an archive
of original sin   captive
in a nether place of our
still-life. God has yet
    to come clean to the fly.

The Finger that Plucks the Lyre Is Not the Song

A far-off voice
is a steeple you'd
crane your neck all day
to catch a glimpse of

*

A temple is a heart
hopeful of being
rewarded
one perfect way

*

Even grief becomes
a beloved friend
difficult
to part from

*

In the aftermath
of a tolled bell
grass and gables attend
to each other again

*

Seen just once
a heron's casual lift-off
you know the lake's
deep readiness

to give up
the very thing
its whole being
craves

*

From the startled buck, from early
snow, from the swallow
that alights briefly
in your life

you learn your own trespass
on affections
that must be allowed
their wild duration

*

Water fleeing a lake accepts
its many fates – to be long married
to islands, to be parted from deserts,
to be displaced in rain

*

Quietly, a river digs in.
Earth allows its own erosion
through a willingness to unite
with the river's winding sūtra

*

Oceans are rivers
that have capitulated.
An island is a blind
whittling

the ocean makes – and being
sometimes a refuge
sometimes a cage –
is terrified of solitude

*

Caged birds
hung world high
are little emperors
summoning note

upon note to fling against
the bamboo bars
a thousand staves,
we call song

     *

A *tanbūra* cannot find
its reason in a single song,
nor exist solely in hope
of a hearing

as consummation
is only a pearl
partway through
love's unravelling

     *

Each day leaves behind a tiny
clear bead. If you do not drink
your fill of sweet water, the well
does not despair

     *

A rosary is both toil
and portent, a heartfelt song
that needs no listener.
Filled already, yet able

to receive, it is undiminished
by distance or departure –
everything gained, a circle
closing without loss

     *

A prayer is a far-off voice
arriving from all ages
that can be unstrung,
but never scattered

Cormorant Fishing

(China)

Black banners in wind – prodded with a pole
fold blade-tight and rip in to the tapestry
of a hunt. Catch still writhing in beaks
they hop back on the sampan, obedient

as old dogs, stay rag-sack still. No quick throw,
or snapping beak in a skyward Y.
The man must grab their rope-thick necks to pry
away the fish and they eat shadows

from their own wings scrap by scrap, small enough
to keep them alive, always the silk-fine
wire in a choke-hold, calling each medallion
to chew at the root of this long hunger, fief

of yellow eye and fish-stare. O flown prayer
hook-hung on a man walking on water.

Whirling Dervish

When you have the air of dervishhood inside,
you will float above the world and there abide

RUMI

A slender axis lancing a white sphere,
the earth's stone weight ravelling from you –

and what I feel most is gravity, the way of a pebble
entering a still pool, living through its own fall,

split from the ripples above, as I watch
you give yourself to air through the night

on a hospital bed, as if sung into a trance, leaving
the world to us, an echo of reed-flute, frenzy of birds,

one small foot grazing the earth, thistledown
or light from the distant polestar

through seafaring, petal fall or wood-smoke,
vague and dissolving by dawn beneath

the spin of your star-trail, a litter
of bone and an angel weeping.

Grasshopper on a Bell Rope

Small purposes
   on eyelash
legs, high-step,
   make little
ground. Felt first,
   the world
is a colossal blister
   of air that
trampolines.
   It hunkers
before air
   hits like a hex,
slung low
   another self
or knot
   on the rope
high-flicking
   and inside
the rolling ring
   forced to kneel
forced to rise rearing
   never lets
go, wisping
   now in a
slowing thresh,
   this quiet
acquiescence
   to gutter
up a wick
   for eons
to a tentative
   nirvana
of the rung-out
   bell

NOTES

Kāma Sūtra (11)
Kāma means sensual or sexual pleasure, and *Sūtra* the thread or line that holds things together. Contrary to popular perception, especially in the western world, *Kāma Sūtra is* not just a sex manual; it discusses love, family life, pleasure, and is presented as a guide to virtuous and gracious living.

Kintsugi (21) and **Ikebana** (64) are Japanese arts embodying the 'Wabi-Sabi' aesthetic, which is influenced by Zen and Mahayana Buddhist philosophy.

Bamboo Flower (23)
It takes decades for a bamboo plant to flower but when it does, the plant dies. In the phenomenon called 'gregarious flowering' entire forests flower and self-destruct at the same time, often triggering famine in rural agrarian communities in India and China.

Satī (24)
Satī, derived from Sanskrit *sat* or 'true essence' has multiple meanings. It is the name of a goddess (first consort of Shiva), and also refers to the ancient practice of self-immolation.

The Fish (26)
Salwar kameez: a traditional dress in India with a flowing tunic and loose, pyjama-like trousers. *Dupatta*: a long multi-purpose scarf that accompanies traditional dress and is a symbol of modesty. *Shiva Lingum* is a phallic representation of the major Hindu deity, Shiva.

Aftersongs (33)
This sequence is based on transcriptions made by Dr Senerat Paranavitana: *Sigiri Graffiti*, vols 1 & 2 (OUP, 1956).

Happy Valley (54)
In colonial Kenya, the 'Happy Valley set' became notorious in the 1930s (up until the Mau Mau uprising) for their hedonistic lifestyle and exploits. These settlers in the Wanjohi valley region east of the Aberdares mountains were mostly British and Irish aristocrats.

How to Watch a Solar Eclipse in a Bowl of Water (59)
Hartal: Indian term for mass protest or civil disobedience. During the JVP insurrection of 1987-89 in Sri Lanka, hartals were enforced by insurgents through violent reprisals. Nightly blackouts were common

and some 25,000 people lost their lives. They were mostly in their teens or early 20s.

Peace (62)
The phenomenon of the 'Grease Devil' (ග්‍රීස් යකා or கிறீஸ் பூதம்) is an actual event of mass hysteria that gripped the country in 2011, soon after the end of the 30-year civil war.

Malum in se (71)
Malum in se: a Latin phrase meaning wrong or evil in itself. This concept was used to identify common-law offences in developing justice systems.